Insan Himalayanoğlu: It's Time to Defect

Abhijit Naskar is a celebrated Neuroscientist, Bestselling Author of 100+ books, and the World's Beloved Poet of 1000+ sonnets, who has been serving at the forefront of humankind's struggle against hate, intolerance, bigotry and fanaticism.

INSAN

Himalayanoğlu

It's Time To Defect

ABHIJIT
NASKAR

Also by Abhijit Naskar

The Art of Neuroscience in Everything
Your Own Neuron: A Tour of Your Psychic Brain
The God Parasite: Revelation of Neuroscience
The Spirituality Engine
Love Sutra: The Neuroscientific Manual of Love
Homo: A Brief History of Consciousness
Neurosutra: The Abhijit Naskar Collection
Autobiography of God: Biopsy of A Cognitive Reality
Biopsy of Religions: Neuroanalysis towards Universal
Tolerance
Prescription: Treating India's Soul
What is Mind?
In Search of Divinity: Journey to The Kingdom of Conscience
Love, God & Neurons: Memoir of a scientist who found
himself by getting lost
The Islamophobic Civilization: Voyage of Acceptance
Neurons of Jesus: Mind of A Teacher, Spouse & Thinker
Neurons, Oxygen & Nanak
The Education Decree
Principia Humanitas
The Krishna Cancer
Rowdy Buddha: The First Sapiens
We Are All Black: A Treatise on Racism
The Bengal Tigress: A Treatise on Gender Equality
Either Civilized or Phobic: A Treatise on Homosexuality
Wise Mating: A Treatise on Monogamy
Illusion of Religion: A Treatise on Religious
Fundamentalism
The Film Testament
Human Making is Our Mission: A Treatise on Parenting
I Am The Thread: My Mission
7 Billion Gods: Humans Above All
Lord is My Sheep: Gospel of Human
Morality Absolute
A Push in Perception
Let The Poor Be Your God
Conscience over Nonsense
Saint of The Sapiens
Time to Save Medicine

Fabric of Humanity
Build Bridges not Walls: In the name of Americana
The Constitution of The United Peoples of Earth
Lives to Serve Before I Sleep
When Humans Unite: Making A World Without Borders
All For Acceptance
Monk Meets World
Mission Reality
Citizens of Peace: Beyond The Savagery of Sovereignty
Operation Justice: To Make A Society That Needs No Law
See No Gender
The Gospel of Technology
Every Generation Needs Caretakers: The Gospel of
Patriotism
Aşkanjali: The Sufi Sermon
Mad About Humans: World Maker's Almanac
Revolution Indomable
When Call The People: My World My Responsibility
No Foreigner Only Family
Hurricane Humans: Give me accountability, I'll give you
peace
Ain't Enough to Look Human
Servitude is Sanctitude
Time To End Democracy: The Meritocratic Manifesto
I Vicdansaadet Speaking: No Rest Till The World is Lifted
Boldly Comes Justice: Sentient not Silent
Good Scientist: When Science and Service Combine
Sleepless for Society
Neden Türk: The Gospel of Secularism
Martyr Meets World: To Solve The Hard Problem of
Inhumanity
The Shape of A Human: Our America Their America
When Veins Ignite: Either Integration or Degradation
Heart Force One: Need No Gun to Defend Society
Solo Standing on Guard: Life Before Law
Generation Corazon: Nationalism is Terrorism
Mucize Insan: When The World is Family
Hometown Human: To Live For Soil and Society
Girl Over God: The Novel
Gente Mente Adelante: Prejudice Conquered is World
Conquered
Earthquakin' Egalitarian: I Die Everyday So Your Children
Can Live
Giants in Jeans: 100 Sonnets of United Earth

Vatican Virus: The Forbidden Fiction (Abi Naskar
Adventures Book 2)
Karadeniz Chronicle: The Novel (Abi Naskar Adventures
Book 3)
Şehit Sevda Society: Even in Death I Shall Live
Handcrafted Humanity: 100 Sonnets For A Blunderful
World
Mücadele Muhabbet: Gospel of An Unarmed Soldier
Making Britain Civilized: How to Gain Readmission to The
Human Race
Dervish Advaitam: Gospel of Sacred Feminines and Holy
Fathers
Honor He Wrote: 100 Sonnets For Humans Not Vegetables
The Gentalist: There's No Social Work, Only Family Work
Either Reformist or Terrorist: If You Are Terror I Am Your
Grandfather
Woman Over World: The Novel (Abi Naskar Adventures
Book 4)
High Voltage Habib: Gospel of Undoctrination
Bulldozer on Duty
Find A Cause Outside Yourself: Sermon of Sustainability
Ingan Impossible: Handbook of Hatebusting
Amor Apocalypse: Canım Sana İhtiyacım
Amantes Assemble: 100 Sonnets of Servant Sultans
Mucize Misafir Merhaba: The Peace Testament
Divane Dynamite: Only truth in the cosmos is love
Sin Dios Sí Hay Divinidad: The Pastor Who Never Was
Corazon Calamidad: Obedient to None, Oppressive to None
Esperanza Impossible: 100 Sonnets of Ethics, Engineering &
Existence
Mukemmel Musalman: Kafir Biraz, Peygamber Biraz
Himalayan Sonneteer: 100 Sonnets of Unsubmission
Yarasistan: My Wounds, My Crown
The Centurion Sermon: Mental Por El Mundo
Her Insan Ailem: Everyone is Family, Everywhere is Home
Humankind, My Valentine: World's First Anthology of 1000
Sonnets
Aşk Mafia: Armor of The World
Vande Vasudhaivam: 100 Sonnets for Our Planetary Pueblo
Visvavictor: Kanima Akiyor Kainat
Sapionova: 200 Limericks for Students
Rowdy Scientist: Handbook of Humanitarian Science

DEDICATION

Dertli olan herkese.

Unutma canım,

*"Güneş kahramandan doğar,
Kahraman doğar karanlıktan."*

CONTENTS

Part 1: Preface

The lines between neuroscience, philosophy, poetry, theology and sociology do not exist in my works. Divisions exist only in the world of amateurs - the deeper you go in mind, the more undivided you become, until you finally realize, it's all one.

It's not enough to outgrow the divisions in culture, we must also outgrow the divisions in intellect.

For example, if you think theology is all about the supernatural, it doesn't mean the entire field of theology is nonsense, it just means, you are studying the wrong kind of theology – you are stuck with an archaic notion of theology. Likewise, if you think science is all about cold facts and figures, then you are studying the wrong kind of science – you are stuck with an archaic notion of science.

Till you develop a common humane ground underneath your feet, all the facts and all the faith won't do you any good.

Part 2: Intro (Turkish)

Merhaba, İnsan ben!
Himalaya evladı,
O yüzden, soyadım,
Himalayanoğlu.

Bazıları bana şair diyo,
Bazıları diyo derviş.
Ben neyim, haberim yok ama,
İnsanız, insan gibi yaşarız.

Müslüman ol,
Hristiyan ol,
Yahudi ol ya da Hindu ol.
Ne istiyorsan ol,
ama herşeyden önce,
iyi bir insan ol.

Bilim adamı, filozof, şair olarak değil,
bu dünyaya ben insan olarak geldim.
İnsan ol, insan kal!
İnsanlıktan başka herşey yalan!

Part 3

Animal we fall, human we fly.
All else save humanity,
is a glorified lie.

Be human, stay human,
To hell with idiotic chatter!
Grounded in heart, guided by brain,
We shall surpass all inhuman clutter.

Curiosity is the lifeforce of sanity,
Superstition is the deathforce of derangement.
Yet superstition passes as otherworldly wisdom,
While common sense is frowned upon as threat.

Curiosidad es vida, hence most live as undead -
It's a new day when we learn something new.
Yesterday I was young, today I am younger -
You grow old when you refuse to learn anew.

Sonnet 1217

Declutter Sonnet

Declutter is the sensible way forward,
So I moved from Windows to Chrome OS.
Less cluttered in mind and machine,
More you shall find the peaceful pace.

Note that I didn't make a mention of iOS,
even though it bears an element of declutter.
Declutter monetized at a ridiculous price tag,
is worse than the most cockeyed clutter.

Declutter and Undisparity, these are
the lifeblood of sustainability.
And there can be no sustainability,
so long as there are vanity and luxury.

Intoxicated by the clutter of luxury,
World chases happiness with no avail.
Health and happiness will come chasing,
Once you learn to live humble and simple.

When you are humble and simple, the entire world knocks on your door to bask in your light. But when you are too full of yourself, one after another you'll keep losing life's most priceless treasures - those that really matter.

Aham brahmandasmi.
意識は宇宙です。
의식은 우주다.
Eres conciencia, eres el cosmos.
Gönül görmezse göz de görmez.

To put all this plainly - consciousness contains the cosmos. Once you feel this in your heart, all the answers, all the solutions, all the light will boldly pour out of your nerves and veins like monsoon rain.

But one thing you must remember -
what the heart doesn't feel,
the eyes cannot see.
And there is no greater obstacle
to vision than rigidity.

Part 4

Youth is a measure of growth, not age -
So long as you are growing, you are young.
The moment you give in to rigidity of age,
Eyes lose sight and heart left unsung.

That's why only the young of mind
can do science,
Science is no feat for the old and rigid.
Science is the spirit of discovery,
Which cannot be harnessed by dead habit.

SCIENCE means Sapient, Conscientious, Infinite Exploration, Never Compromising Empathy. Here what I am pointing at is this - the glare of unscrupulous science is more dangerous than the darkness of ignorance.

The most commonly understandable example that comes to mind, is that of Artificial Intelligence - or to be particular - Generative AI.

Sonnet 1218

AI Deception
(The Sonnet)

Anybody can be a singer using Autotune,
Using ChatGPT anybody can be a writer.
But I'm yet to find an AI that can compose,
Love thy neighbor, or love has no gender.

Yet the problem is, neither human
nor AI can detect AI generation.
The world is already being flooded
with soulless, deceitful creation.

In the midst of such grave misgivings,
Honor alone can bring illumination.
Before you place anyone on pedestal,
Observe character beyond the creation.

Even I use photoshop, to enhance my covers,
But the words beneath are unvarnished Naskar.
AI can be a great help if you know how to
use it honorably, so originality is empowered.

It's quite simple really. There is nothing more dangerous than ethicless tech. Science is the supreme force of change - it can be an instrument of creation or a weapon of mass destruction, depending on the tendencies of the hands that wield it.

Part 5

Sonnet 1219

Humanitarian Behaviorism
(The Sonnet)

Give me a drop of love,
I'll shower you with monsoon.
Hit me with loads of hate,
I'll silently disappear soon.

I don't approve of hate in return,
I just walk away from wrong done to me.
Wrong done to another is another matter,
I am the bulldozer, if you are the bully.

I am a biologist and behaviorist after all,
I don't need to do harm to restrain harm.
Weaknesses of the apes are my common knowledge,
Where there is brain, there's no need for brawn.

Brain used to lift the world,
is the only human brain.
All else is mindless protoplasm,
ever-consumed with greed and gain.

Soneto del
Visvavencedor

No soy poeta,
Soy un paradigma.
No soy religioso,
Soy divinidad viva.

Más que un científico,
Soy la brújula para ciencia.
Más que un filósofo barato,
Soy el epítome de la armonía.

No soy ni policía ni político,
Soy la tierra del orden sin ley.
Soy la campaña de un mundo de luz,
Más allá de la fiesta de la muerte.

Yo soy el visva (mundo), yo soy vencedor.
Para el dolor humano, humano salvador.

Part 6

Sonnet 1220

I do my writing in the dark,
That's when I feel most bright.
That's when my light pours out,
That's when I feel beyond fright.

However, I am not a writer,
Writers suffer from writer's block.
I suffer from overflow if anything,
Pouring words don't let me doze off.

One heart, one brain, one backbone -
that's all it takes to change the world.
When all three boil with vigor of life,
you can barely sit still avoiding effort.

To lift the world is a labor of love,
Still it strikes strain on mind at times.
That's where reformer stands out in crowd,
No strain clouds long a mission-driven mind.

Sonnet 1221

Mission is purpose magnified,
Purpose is potential focused,
Potential is protoplasm evolving,
Protoplasm is a pocket universe.

There is not one but two universe,
One of mind, one of matter.
The one we see is born of mind,
While we are oblivious of the other.

Perception is not a reflection of reality,
Reality is the reflection of perception.
We only see what we're inclined to see,
The inconvenient escapes all assumption.

Truth is the biggest lie of all,
All truths are rooted in assumption.
In fact, real truth isn't a stagnant point,
But a dynamic force of eternal correction.

Sonnet 1222

Truth isn't a measure of knowledge,
Truth is the measure of correction.
Light isn't a measure of illumination,
Light is the measure of intention.

Education isn't an exercise in learning,
Education is an exercise in unlearning.
To educate, one must first uneducate
of all assumptions one's been believing.

Fear and education don't go together,
Where there is fear there is no learning.
Problem is, fear is never peddled as fear,
More often fear is disguised as discipline.

There can be no growth without discipline,
But reckless discipline just as crippling.

43

Part 7

Life begins where death ends,
Death ends where fear fades.
Fear fades where vision reigns,
Vision reigns where apathy ends.

Apathy, apathy, apathy - that's the trouble with this world - reckless, mindless, brainless exploits of apathy.

However, let's go a little deeper, shall we!

Narcissism has a time and place, cold detachment has a time and place. Problem is, we've made a world out of narcissism and detachment, while hypocritically diagnosing them as clinical on one hand, and sugarcoating them as self-care or stoicism on the other. In reality, it's all nonsense. When people are upset at you, with no fault of your own, or when they come to take away your dream, that's when you gotta let detachment kick on. Likewise, when shallow nitwits commit harm in front of your eyes, that's when you gotta exercise your narcissism, and treat them like a parent would treat their child when they've done something wrong. Even the ugliest of animal faculty can be used for good, when wielded with conscience. It's about using the whole of your mind, rather than giving in to all the prehistoric intellectual dualities of narcissism and altruism, or attachment and detachment. When people are helpless, to them be a christ - but when they behave heartless instead, be the light to their lies.

To put it simply, you gotta adjust your behavior as per the requirements of the situation. Where humility is needed, be humble - where confidence is called for, grow big as a dinosaur. Only one kind of thought, emotion and behavior does not apply to varied circumstances of life - you must learn to be flexible. Be bold where needed, be cold where needed - speak the truth where needed, keep the truth where needed.

Part 8

INSAN HIMALAYANOĞLU: IT'S TIME TO DEFECT

When I wanna pen something extremely personal, without actually revealing anything, I just write it in spanish or turkish. If you wanna study the mountain, study the mainstream work - but if you wanna learn about the person, study the turkish and spanish portion of my work.

That's why most of the titles of my works are in turkish or spanish - because I can't write a single word unless I feel the title boiling in my blood - and although English is unofficially the first language of earth, because of its savage imperialist history, it is neither the profoundest nor the most beautiful language on earth.

Does that mean, we should wipe out english from the world altogether? Of course not - that would be yet another boneheaded exercise in bigotry and intolerance. Instead, what's really needed is a genuine humane intention to create a truly magnificent multilingual society - towards a multicultural world. Learn to look beyond the puny confines of one petty language, because the world is too grand to be wasted in the gutter of one language and one culture. Every culture is my culture, every country is mine - defiant descendants of divided ancestors, hand in hand we shall fly.

Part 9

Neden bu kadar çok konuşuyorum,
Yalnızım, yalnız kalacağım!
Her zaman herkese gülümsüyorum ama,
İçimde gözyaşlarımla savaşacağım.

Bolca bilgelik dağıttım,
Ama kimse bana söylemedi,
Yazmayı bırak, sarıl bana!
Gözyaşlar senin, benim olsun,
Gülüşler benim, verdim sana.

Give me your tears, take my cheer.
Give me your sigh, take my high.

Art of Linguistics
(Sonnet 1223)

No language speaks of freedom better than spanish,
No language speaks of love better than turkish,
No language speaks of oneness better than sanskrit,
No language interprets better than our good ol' english.

No language speaks to computers better than code,
No language speaks of matter better than physics.
No language speaks of mind better than neurology,
No language speaks pattern better than mathematics.

No language speaks of thought better than philosophy,
No language speaks of emotion better than poetry.
No language speaks of justice better than sociology,
No language speaks of behavior better than psychology.

Purpose of language is communication not argumentation,
If it doesn't bridge the cliffs it all brings but extinction.

Languages are but echoes of each other,
Based on the environment each feels unique.
No language is superior, no language is inferior,
All are born of human mind to meet at heart's peak.

Language and ideology are not the same thing. Sociology is a language, socialism is an ideology - economics is a language, capitalism is an ideology. Language is an act of communication, ideology is an act of miscommunication. Focus on the language, not the ideology. Because no matter how perfect an ideology appears to be, sooner or later all ideology gets corrupt, particularly because ideology thrives on rigidity - whereas all languages evolve with time at a simple, natural, and almost seamless pace, with no reliance on allegiance and popularity.

Part 10

INSAN HIMALAYANOĞLU: IT'S TIME TO DEFECT

The point is this. Potential and evolution go together. Whatever has potential, evolves - whatever evolves, has potential.

Potential never dies, it only changes shape. Take radio for example. Radio never died, it evolved into podcast - just like television never died, it just evolved into streaming.

However, just like everything old is not gold, everything new is not necessarily cool, particularly if you don't know the meaning of the word "moderation". I had to cancel my netflix subscription after using it only for a couple of days, because the sheer volume of content was way overwhelming and ridiculously distracting and stupefying (for Naskar that is).

Besides, I rarely like new shows and movies anyway - I keep digging up old radio dramas and tv shows from the 80's and earlier – which I keep running in the background while I am writing.

Anyway, the point is this.

Distraction is the enemy of creativity - if you wanna be creative, discard all unnecessary thrills and distractions from your life. If you wanna do something that nobody has done before, first learn to live like nobody has lived before.

Part 11

Sonnet 1224

Simplicity seats profundity,
Complexity contains shallowness.
Lavishness indicates thievishness,
Luxury facilitates pettiness.

Genius writers write simple,
Garbage writers write fancy.
Wise humans live simple,
Dumb apes live in luxury.

Move past the lure of packaging,
Focus on the potential within.
Use the packaging as per purpose,
Never confuse purpose with packaging.

Hardwork adorns the human,
Luxury adorns the ape.
In thirst, a glass of water is priceless,
Not a thousand pricy wine crates.

Lower the animal, fancier the extravagance,
Fancy car, fancy clothes, fancy mansion.
Higher the human, simpler the existence,
Simple life orchestrates mindful ascension.

I don't approve of anything fancy - whether it comes from intellectualism or anti-intellectualism. If I've said once, I've said a thousand times - I can entertain anything that facilitates welfare, but nothing that peddles narrowness and shallowness.

The point is this.

I am not an atheist, I am the Everest. Atheism is focused on the nonexistence of God, and the supreme significance of facts - my focus is neither. My focus is on the better existence of humans. To me, human welfare is of supreme significance - I couldn't care less whether there is a sentient almighty or not. What I say is simple - GOD means Guts On Duty. It has nothing to do with the supernatural, and everything to do with the natural accountability of natural mortals.

Spangskritlish
(Sonnet for Tomorrow's Citizen)

Jagrata, uttistha, jagat skandhe grhana,
Atmanam vismaratu, samsarasya asrumarjayatu.
Dvesam himsam ca sarvam parityajya,
Jagrata, uttistha, sumanusya bhavatu.

Eres Dios, eres diablo -
Lo que decidas, ¡así será!
Human destiny is human decision,
Somos la iluminación en toda oscuridad.

We are the illumination,
We are the answer to our prayer.
Karanlık bile korkacak bizden,
When we rise as each other's keeper.

Dolor del mundo es nuestro dolor.
While the apes doze, human builds the road.

Part 12

Computer to Consciousness
(Sonnet 1225)

To me arabic is just as sweet as sanskrit,
Spanish is just as passionate as turkish.
I can't give up one to butter the other,
I am the sun, I need all the skies.

Once upon a time at my university dorm,
They used to gather around to hear me mumble.
So I had to put my coding assignment aside,
I loved machines, more I loved workings mental.

Through a rollercoaster ride of uncharted ocean,
Engineer became monk, monk emerged scientist.
Despite the thrill of building cars and rockets,
I feel more alive in being the human bridge.

Thus goes the odyssey of the bulldozer on duty.
Before we innovate tech, we gotta renovate humanity.

Sonnet 1226

Every mind is a bridge,
Every mind is a wall.
Choice is yours, what you be,
New human or mistake ancestral!

Surrender to no one,
neither god nor government!
You are born to move the world,
not to be immobilized
by halfbaked commandment.

No law is impeccable,
No scripture is absolute.
Constructs born of human mind,
Require scrutiny not salute.

Surrender only to love,
Directed at the living.
Scripture, constitution, all are toys,
True light comes from mind in churning.

Part 13

Love Before Language
(Sonnet 1227)

'Aezam alhaqiqat hi alhubu ,
'Aezam qanun hu alhab.
'Aezam 'iiman hu alhubu ,
'Aezam wujud hu alhab.

Premasatyam brahmasatyam,
Prema vina astitvam nasti.
Premadarsanam brahmadarsanam,
Prema vina brahmandam nasti.

Love happens regardless of facts,
Facts happen regardless of love.
When love and facts come together,
Magic happens in our veins and nerve.

Love before language,
Heart before heritage.
To unify this broken world,
I once took the divine pledge.

Part 14

I am beyond prejudice,
not because I'm a genius.
I am beyond prejudice,
because I am a human.

I am beyond intolerance,
not because I'm a scientist.
I am beyond intolerance,
because I am a human.

I am beyond hate,
not because I am a poet.
I am beyond hate,
because I am a human.

Sonnet 1228

Writers suffer from writer's block,
I suffer from eternal deluge.
No matter how much I don't wanna write,
Words don't allow me a moment's snooze.

I toss, I turn,
trying to keep the noise out.
Yet I can't seem to fall asleep,
till I write it all down.

Sometimes the burden is too heavy
for a simple mortal brain.
This cosmic heart is too grand
to be contained by a mortal brain.

Cosmos comes from consciousness,
Consciousness comes from cosmos.
Conscious life is cosmic life,
All else is counterfeit glasnost.

Part 15

Ev-siz evlilik yok.
İnsan otelden ayrılabilir,
Ama evden vazgeçmek yok.

Benimde hayalim var,
Seninle bir ev kurmak istiyorum.
Sen nerde, evim orda,
Sensiz ben evimi bulamıyorum.

Hotels are for leaving,
Home is for returning.

Companies make trade,
Companion makes treasure.
Materials make a mess,
Memories make cheer.

I looked for love,
I found pain.
I avoided pain,
I lost love.

I looked for pain,
I found love.
I accepted pain,
I discovered joy.

Aşkı aradım,
Acıları buldum.
Acıları terkettim,
Aşkı kaybettim.

Acıları aradım,
Aşkı buldum.
Acılara sarıldım,
Saadetimi buldum.

Buscando amor,
Encontré dolor.
Evitando dolor,
Perdí el amor.

Buscando dolor,
Encontre amor.
Aceptando dolor,
Me levanté amador.

Part 16

All through history we've branded night as evil, but the fact of the matter is, night is the best time for healing. When there is no judgment, no noise, no cacophony of cockeyed condescension - when there is nothing but sheer emptiness, that's when we heal. (That's why I write during the night, and sleep during the day.)

Güneş kahramandan doğar,
Kahraman doğar karanlıktan.
Yaralardan yangın doğar,
Bilgelik doğar bulutlardan.

Clouds are but herald of wisdom,
Resist the clouds, you resist monsoon.
There is no shortcut to life and lift,
Chasing shortcuts wisdom becomes wool.

Churn your heart, churn your soul,
Till the soil till you reach your goal.
There is no shortcut to success,
Look for shortcut, you'll end up in hole.

İnsan amaçsız olamaz,
Amaç insansız.
İnsan vicdansız olamaz,
Vicdan insansız.

Conscienceless character cannot be,
Characterless conscience cannot be.
Civilizationless human cannot be,
Humanless civilization cannot be.

Civilization is not a destination,
Civilization is the journey.
Heaven is a people, not a place,
An exercise in attachment, not apathy.

There's a terrorist in all of us,
as well as a transformer.
Decision is totally yours,
Wreak havoc or rise a reformer.

Part 17

Reform is not an exercise in intellect,
Reform is an exercise of the whole being.
You need head, you need heart, and a backbone,
Only then your life will be socially uplifting.

Society is not your obligation,
Society is your salvation.
Exist as proof of the best
of humanity, or don't exist at all.

Say to yourself -
I shall exist as the pinnacle
of human capacity, or not at all.

I shall exist as the pinnacle
of capacity, courage
and conscience, or not at all.

Ama, kaybediyorum ya,
gücümü kaybediyorum -
İstemiyorum artık,
artık yazmak istemiyorum.

Duymuyorsun beni -
bir söz daha yalnız
yazmak istemiyorum artık.

Just as I hit rock bottom,
I remember, "my life is not mine."
Lo, and behold motivation dawns,
Piercing all fracture of mind!

Greatest motivation is self-motivation.
Greatest awareness is self-awareness.
Greatest correction is self-correction.

Manufacture your own motivation,
Chart your own correction.
Take charge of your own morality,
The journey is the destination.

Sonnet 1229

No matter the pollution around,
Lungs never forget to breathe.
No matter the hate and judgment around,
How could the heart forget to love!

The sun never forgets to rise,
No matter the stubbornness of the night.
No matter the dampness in the world,
Why should the neurons forget to light!

No matter the wind most treacherous,
The trees never forget to grow.
No matter the pressure outside,
Why should the backbone bend down low!

Monsoon comes every time,
defying all evident drought.
Whole world will lose its sight,
if one bold heart forgets to sprout.

Part 18

Time is love, love is time -
Tiempo es amor, amor es tiempo.
Her saat sevda saatidir,
Humano es amor, amor humano.

Everybody comes of age,
Very few come alive.
Everybody lies in deathbed,
Very few are ever out of it.

It's stupid to have a tool
and never use it,
but stupider still is to have
a life and never live it.

It's stupid to have a brain
and never use it,
but stupider still is to have
a heart never heed it.

Sonnet 1230

Naskaristan, The Sonnet

Where no one cries of hunger,
For neighbor comes before netflix,
No one needs bulletproof backpacks,
For children come before profits,

Where women can pursue their dreams,
Without being castrated by masculinity,
Where a mother can feed her child,
Without attracting prehistoric insecurity,

Where love isn't chained to archaic texts,
For reform triumphs over rigidity,
Where all colors make the rainbow of life,
For life isn't chained to no ideology,

Where reason outshines all superstition,
Heartland beyond hateland is Naskaristan.

Sonnet 1231

There is a land within the lands,
which is a land beyond the lands,
an interior, past exterior divide,
beyond all primitive shenanigans.

In that land love reigns supreme,
never entertaining bookish division.
It's a world of sentient acceptance,
tempered by the torrents of reason.

For the ape in me,
Time is the movement of fear.
For the human I am,
Time is but the march of a lover.

(Para el mono en mí,
El tiempo es la moción del miedo.
Para el humano soy,
El tiempo es el avance de un amador.)

All originality originates from you,
From you emerges all direction.
Take stock of your backbone's resolve,
March ahead bold, and mark your salvation.

Part 19

Sonnet 1232

Once upon a time Marvel made sense,
Today Marvel manufactures cheap noise.
Once upon a time twitter was relevant,
Today it is plain obsolete and pointless.

No wonder I have slowed down greatly,
As I transcended records 'n races long ago.
I could now stop writing altogether,
I don't, 'cause it keeps me from the low.

Years back I made a promise to myself,
Once I've published 100 books I'd be happy.
Yet here I am way past 100,
And I realize, in struggle lies serenity.

The stupid keep on blabbering,
just to make a lot of noise,
while the wise knows to adopt silence,
when they have nothing more to say.

In time be a chatterbox,
When no need, adopt silence.
Speech and time both are golden,
When applied in right time 'n place.

Words can aid revolution,
Words can wreak havoc.
Words can lift up the world,
Words can shove it in the muck.

Be aware of your words and thoughts,
Be aware of their rightful place.
Scrutinize yourself before you speak,
Let no impulse pass without conscience.

All constitutions are mere books,
All scriptures are mere books,
Even my books are mere books.

Nothing is above scrutiny,
Nothing is infallible.
Till you get this simple fact,
No society is reparable.

Repair takes resilience,
Rigidity takes none.
Repair is an act of life,
Rigidity is life gone wrong.

Sharpen the eraser of conscience,
Use it despite your comforting insecurity.
Correction is more important than tradition,
Correction brings progress, not conformity.

Those who can correct themselves,
Need no other teacher and guide.
Those who recognize the light within,
Are no longer dependent on external light.

It's okay to fall apart - those who
never fall apart, never fly afar.
If you are tired, slow down, don't back down -
Occasional breaks empower one to persevere.

The light is always there inside you,
Sometimes exhaustion casts a shadow.
Occasional resets are crucial for the journey,
Thus your eyes once again start to glow.

Part 20

Sonnet 1233

Favoritism is Good
(The Sonnet)

My favorite language in the world is Turkish,
Because its culture electrifies my scars.
My favorite language in the East is Telugu,
Because its music emboldens my nerves.

My favorite language in the West is Spanish,
Because it teaches me the worth of freedom.
Favorite ancient tongues are Arabic 'n Sanskrit,
For one embodies peace, another assimilation.

My favorite science of all is electronics,
For it empowers my imagination untainted.
My favorite philosophy is everyday curiosity,
It helps me transcend all sectarian intellect.

My favorite religion in the world is service,
Because it transforms an animal into human.
I don't care what you believe or don't,
As long as your behavior speaks compassion.

Favoritism is a civilized faculty,
when practiced beyond blood and border.
Problem is when you see nothing at all,
beyond the rim of your family and culture.

I Am My Teacher
(Sonnet 1234)

I teach myself when I need to learn something,
I correct myself when I make mistakes.
No two year old shaped as 40, 50, 60 or 70,
Has the maturity to provide me moral guidance.

I taught myself electronics when I fell for it,
I taught myself music in my youthful high.
I taught myself languages in sheer obsession,
I taught myself aeronautics when I wanted to fly.

Critics mail, I should add "biggest ego" to my bio,
I thank them all for an astounding revelation.
If I actually behaved befitting my capacity,
Half your legends will lose their reputation.

You only see the tip of the ice-berg,
Fullness of the Himalayas you'll never see.
I chose to put many of my passions aside,
One path, one mission - one answer to calamity.

Part 21

All The World's An Asylum
(Sonnet 1235)

All the world's an asylum,
All the people are lunatics.
Some are but loonies of love,
Some loonies run by prejudice.

Some die running in love of currency,
Some die sharing the currency of love.
Beyond the grasp of dollar and euro,
Love is the only nonvolatile
currency in the world.

It's good to be a loonie,
If the reason is justly humane.
When human welfare is at stake,
It's only logical to be insane.

Sane, insane - be as the need arises,
To hell with the judgment of nitwits!
In an organic world no sanity is absolute,
Boldly walk the spectrum as the purpose fits.

Part 22

Absolution is fiction,
Only evolution is real.
Either improve or don't,
There is no perfection surreal.

Perfection is a primeval lie,
Only animals seek comfort in inaction.
Flawlessness is the cover for indifference,
It has nothing to do with civilized ascension.

Correction is ascension,
Perfection is evaporation.
Correction is existence,
Perfection is castration.

In the kingdom of animals,
nothing is a flaw,
hence nothing needs correction.
Flaw is a human construct,
meant to instigate correction.

Put simply, perfection is animal, correction is human.
Understand this simple fact, you'll learn to be human.

Todo el mundo es un manicomio,
Toda la gente está loca.
Algunos locos, porque enamorados,
Algunos venden intolerancia.

Better drunk in love
than sober in indifference.
Better sober in humility
than drunk with arrogance.

Drunk or sober, words are irrelevant,
Burn all words and stand your ground.
Words may contain puny intellectuals,
They fall short to define a mind unbound.

However, I must make something clear.

I am not asking you to replace
intellectualism with mysticism,
nor am I asking you to replace
mysticism with intellectualism.
For once in your life,
stand as a whole human being,
submit no more to tribal dualism.

Part 23

This ism and that ism have turned the world into a prison. All isms are illusion, as such, none of them should be taken seriously. And definitely no ism must ever - I repeat - ever be placed in a position to dictate life, because birth of each ism is rooted in a handicap - different kinds of handicap, but handicap no less.

Yet that handicap or illusion, never manifests as such, instead they all manifest as a form of augmented perception - some sort of higher knowledge, if you may.

But here's the thing.

Person becomes great by working hard for their mission, not by bowing lazily to an illusion. If an illusion helps you work harder, and cope with difficulty, then by all means keep it, but never for a moment let any illusion paralyze your footsteps with baseless fear or indifference-inducing hope.

What you believe or don't to cope with difficulty, is completely up to - you have to answer to no one - but the moment any belief induces rigidity, it must be questioned - and it must be questioned by you, before anyone else.

The question of belief has nothing to do with rationality, and everything to do with rigidity. Belief is a matter of sentiment, which transcends the mechanistic grasp of rationality. Sentiment rationalized is sentiment ruined.

Let me put this into perspective.

I am yet to find a happy computer, despite being the epitome of rationality. Likewise, I am yet to find a civilized animal, despite being the epitome of sentimentality. What this means is that, only with the right balance between rationality and sentimentality there can exist a magical creature called human, brimming with infinite potential - but mess up the balance, and you are stuck with either a cold mechanical world run by rationality or a red-hot uncivilized world run by brutality - both equally unfit for preserving civilized life.

Part 24

You must learn to pace the spectrum of perception as widely as you can - adjust your inclinations according to the requirements of time and circumstances. Mark you, I am not talking about making compromise. I am talking about, using your full capacity as a human being, rather than being a mindless mouthpiece for this ism and that ism, or this culture and that culture.

No allegiance - period.

If you must pledge allegiance, pledge it to the cause of expansion. Expansion alone can ensure true uplift, both for the individual as well as the collective.

In doing so, you'll have to spend a great deal of time in darkness - it's alright. Befriend the darkness, my friend! Walk to the length and breadth of the night, and all fear will disappear into thin air.

Remember this.

Explorers of night are emperors of the day, explorers of chaos are emperors of order. Either fear the sea, and you'll have to spend your cowardly life as slave on the shore, or venture into the sea boldly, and you shall return to the shore as emperor - and not just any emperor, but egalitarian emperor - not just any sultan, but servant sultan. Because that's the only kind of civilized emperor there is - that's the only kind of civilized sultan there is.

Part 25

Civilization is a majestic blend of sentiment and reason - yet in our mechanical stupidity, we've put all our attention on reason - as a result, such reason has only amplified the predominant disparities of society, instead of alleviating them.

Take everyday ordinary decency out of the equation, and all your intellectual prowess in various fields will only make those fields colder and colder - until the entire world gets so freezing cold that you could barely recollect how it feels to live in a warm human world.

Is this what you want! Is this the best substitute for the jungle you can think of! If that's the case, then why the hell did we step out of the jungle in the first place!

If all we wanted was to create just a different kind of jungle, then what was so wrong with life in nature's green jungle! At least it was honest. An honest life in the jungle is far better than a hypocrite's life in society. Put it simpler still - an honest animal is far more civilized than a hypocrite human.

What is this hypocrisy, one wonders! Is it merely dishonesty, or is there much more to it than that! Indeed there is. Because here the dishonesty is not merely about some trivial falsehood - it's about an entire existence founded on falsehood - the falsehood of human identity.

When all our perception of human identity is rooted in something so childish as appearance, it is anything but an identity. Behavior makes identity, not appearance. As a result, what we have in the world is an animal species living a delusion – a delusion that they are human, just because they look human.

To serve is to be human,
To love is to be human.
To help is to be human,
To heal is to be human.

Now ask yourself, is that the case on planet earth!

Part 26

Vakit varsa sev,
Zaman varsa sev.
Hayat varsa sev,
Nefes varsa sev.

Aklın varsa düşün,
Kalbin varsa hisset.
Gözlerin varsa gör,
Ellerin varsa yardım et.

If you have a brain, think,
If you have a heart, feel.
If you have ears, listen,
If you have eyes, open and see.

Part 27

Now let's move from love amongst all to love between two, for a moment.

Fall in love as many times as you want, as young as you want, but never marry young, only to take the easy way out. Love is an act of eternal duty - there is no way out. You can never be a vessel of love, till you cut ties with all convenient escape routes. Sure, there may be exceptions, but you for one stand your ground.

Let the other choose the escape route if they so desire - accept their wish as their chosen path to happiness - but you for one, must never, I repeat, never initiate escape yourself.

There is no escape in love -
till you get this, you ain't no lover.
And if you ain't no lover, you ain't alive.

Curves don't sustain love -
absolute, inescapable attachment does.

Those who look for a relationship,
don't care about abs and racks.
Those who look for abs and racks,
don't care for relationship.

Relationship founded on
appearance is transaction,
relationship founded on
attachment is a promise.
And it is far better to lose
your life than break a promise.

You know why?

Because -

Existence is an exercise in promise -
if the promise fades, so will you.
Life is an act of promise -
Promise broken is life untrue.

Let others break their promise as they choose,
True character is rooted in promise and principles.
Either make a promise or do not ever,
But never you abandon your duty in the middle.

I'll put it to you plainly.
Once you commit yourself to someone,
their welfare becomes your responsibility for life.

137

Part 28

Sonnet 1236

Lyubimaya
(The Sonnet)

I am happy - I am happy
to see that you are happy.
May they give you all the joy,
Of which you dreamt with me.

I was just a struggling autodidact,
yet to be the legend I made myself.
How was I supposed to settle down,
in the balkans with white picket fence!

Partners with infinite patience,
only ever exist in fairytales.
Yet I feel no grudge whatsoever,
as they're happy with their choice.

There's a divine bliss in being dumped,
at least one is no longer a burden.
Purpose of love is to see another happy,
not to sentence them to life-imprisonment.

Part 29

Sonnet 1237

Selfless love is the only love I know,
All other love are capitalist merchandise.
Dating market has become a stock market,
Expectations encapsulated in hypocritical lies.

For the world to have true love,
You must become true love.
Yours is not to pretend and lie,
Yours is to but love and die.

Expectations are a crucial part of relationship,
But they must never become the driving force.
Love, because you don't know any other way to live,
If it isn't reciprocated, don't drown in remorse.

Love is the only way,
all else is futile.
Pain of love is pearl of love,
all else is vain and vile.

Part 30

Only love can bring full freedom, all else brings half freedom. What is half freedom you ask? When in the name of freedom you imprison yourself to one side or sect, everything outside that sect seems evil. For example, fundamentalists choose the side of blind faith, and every act of reason seems like blasphemy - just like cold, sharp-tongue intellectuals choose the side of rationality even at the expense of humanity, and everything illogical seems outdated - or wait, I got a better one - so-called social activists often get so attached to their self-imposed identity of victimhood, that every person with a political, corporate, legal or bureaucratic background seems to appear as devil incarnate. This, my friend, is what I call "half freedom", which by the way, is far worse than the lack of freedom. And even though it manifests as an act of willful choice, when you get down to it, it's just plain old rigidity. And if we want to build a truly just, inclusive and progressive society, this hypocritical half-freedom won't do - what's needed is whole freedom - a kind of freedom that liberates the mind of all superstition as well as ignorant suspiciousness. It's time we realize, yelling about justice without using common sense is just as useless as keeping quiet. What this means is that, we gotta come together regardless of our background - the teacher, the scientist, the student, the copper, the politician, the civil servant, the entrepreneur, the economist, the janitor, the construction worker - every single person from every single walk of life must come forward surpassing all suspicious conspiracy, and contribute the best of their capacity in the making of a real civilized world.

Part 31

No trust, no civilization - just like, no reason, no civilization. So how do we decide when to trust and when to practice reason!

That's the whole point, isn't it! That's the whole point of how human you are!

It seems such a herculean task because of all the garbage rigidity that you've let fester in your mind. Destroy all rigidity, and all the necessary insight will appear on its own. It's the rigidity that stands between you and the insight, nothing else. Bring down the rigidity and the bridge will appear - quite naturally. Just like, as soon as the clouds fade, like magic the sun appears.

What this means is that, the sun is always there - you don't see it, because of the clouds. And in case of the mind, rigidity covers the consciousness with clouds. Throw all rigidity in the trash and consciousness will shine like a beacon, lighting the way for both the individual and the society. But try to find a way without first acknowledging and removing the rigidity, and you're destined to be stuck in the whirlpool of self-imposed ignorance and savagery. Remember this - replacing one prison with another, is not freedom, it's regression.

You gotta be free from the obsession of freedom, only then you'll be really free. Because the obsession of freedom is extremely deceitful, and more importantly, it's extremely addictive. Hence, as you get hooked on the rush of rebellion, you start rebelling like a mindless savage just for the sake of rebellion.

The obsession of freedom peddles only persecution complex, which does nothing to make the mind free - quite the contrary, it depresses the mind further, so that it revolts even more, quite aimlessly. And there is nothing more animal than a human mind revolting at the wrong places, and more importantly, at the wrong people.

That's why I say, you gotta defect - you gotta defect from ideology - not this ideology and that ideology, but every ideology. You gotta defect from the entire rotten circus of sectarianism - only then you shall find freedom - only then you shall find civilization - only then you shall be human.

153

BIBLIOGRAPHY

Archer M., (2000), Being Human: The Problem of Agency. Cambridge University Press.

Adolphs R (2003) Cognitive neuroscience of human social behaviour. Nature Rev Neurosci 4: 165–178.

Adolphs R, Tranel D, Damasio AR (2003) Dissociable neural systems for recognizing emotions. Brain Cogn 52: 61–69.

Andresen, Jensine, and Robert Forman, eds. Cognitive Models and Spiritual Maps. Bowling Green, Ohio: Imprint Academic, 2000.

Bernstein R.J., (1971), Praxis and Action: Contemporary Philosophies of Human Activity. Philadelphia: University of Pennsylvania Press.

Bernstein R.J., (1976), The Restructuring Social and Political Thought.

Bogen, J.E.(1995a), 'On the neurophysiology of consciousness: Part I. An overview', Consciousness and Cognition, 4.

Bogen, J.E. (1995b), 'On the neurophysiology of consciousness: Part II. Constraining the semantic problem', Consciousness and Cognition, 4.

Bremner, J. D., R. Soufer, et al. (2001). "Gender differences in cognitive and neural correlates of remembrance of emotional words." Psychopharmacol Bull 35 (3).

Brothers, L. (2002). The social brain: A project for integrating primate behavior and neurophysiology in a new domain. In J. T. Cacioppo et al. (Eds.), Foundations in neuroscience. Cambridge, MA: MIT Press.

Buss, D. D. (2003). Evolutionary Psychology: The New Science of Mind, 2nd ed. New York: Allyn & Bacon.

Buss, D. M. (1989). "Conflict between the sexes: Strategic interference and the evocation of anger and upset." J Pers Soc Psychol 56 (5).

Buss, D. M. (1995). "Psychological sex differences. Origins through sexual selection." Am Psychol 50 (3).

Buss, D. M., and D. P. Schmitt (1993). "Sexual strategies theory: An evolutionary perspective on human mating." Psychol Rev 100 (2).

Chomsky Noam, (2016) Who Rules the World?

Churchland, P.S. (1986), Neurophilosophy (Cambridge, MA: The MIT Press).

Churchland, P.S. & Ramachandran, V.S. (1993), 'Filling in: Why Dennett is wrong', in Dennett and His Critics:

Demystifying Mind, ed. B. Dahlbom (Oxford: Blackwell Scientific Press).

Churchland, P.S., Ramachandran, V.S. & Sejnowski, T.J. (1994), 'A critique of pure vision', in Large- scale Neuronal Theories of the Brain, ed. C. Koch & J.L. Davis (Cambridge, MA: The MIT Press).

Crick, F. (1994), The Astonishing Hypothesis: The Scientific Search for the Soul (New York: Simon and Schuster).

Crick, F. (1996), 'Visual perception: rivalry and consciousness', Nature, 379.

Crick, F. & Koch, C. (1992), 'The problem of consciousness', Scientific American, 267.

d'Aquili, Eugene. "Senses of Reality in Science and Religion." Zygon 17, no 4 (1982)

d'Aquili, Eugene. "The Biopsychological Determinants of Religious Ritual Behavior." Zygon 10, no. 1 (1975)

d'Aquili, Eugene. "The Myth-Ritual Complex: A Biogenetic Structural Analysis." Zygon 18, no. 3 (1983)

d'Aquili, Eugene, and Andrew Newberg. The Mystical Mind: Probing the Biology of Religious Experience. Minneapolis: Fortress Press, 1999.

Damasio, A. (1994) Descartes' Error: Emotion, Reason and the Human Brain. New York, Putnams.

Damasio, A. (1999) The Feeling of What Happens: Body, Emotion and the Making of Consciousness. London, Heinemann.

Darwin, C. (1859) On the Origin of Species by Means of Natural Selection. London, Murray.

Darwin, C. (1871) The Descent of Man and Selection in Relation to Sex. London, John Murray.

Dawkins, R. (1976) The Selfish Gene. Oxford, Oxford University Press; a new edition, with additional material, was published in 1989.

Dewhurst, Kenneth, and A. W. Beard. "Sudden Religious Conversions in Temporal Lobe Epilepsy." British Journal of Psychiatry 117 (1970)

Dewhurst K, Beard AW. Sudden religious conversions in temporal lobe epilepsy. 1970 Epilepsy Behav 2003

Devinsky O, Lai G. Spirituality and religion in epilepsy. Epilepsy Behav 2008.

E. Horvitz, "One Hundred Year Study on Artificial Intelligence: Reflections and Framing," ed: Stanford University, 2014.

Eckhart Meister, Selected Writings

Farah, M.J. (1989), 'The neural basis of mental imagery', Trends in Neurosciences, 10.

Freud, S. "Selected papers on hysteria and other psychoneuroses" Journal of Nervous and Mental Disease 1909.

Freud, S. "The Origin and Development of Psychoanalysis", 1910

Freud, S. "Psychopathology of everyday life", 1914

Freud, S. "Beyond the Pleasure Principle", 1920

Frith, C.D. & Dolan, R.J. (1997), 'Abnormal beliefs: Delusions and memory', Paper presented at the May, 1997, Harvard Conference on Memory and Belief.

Gay, Volney, ed. Neuroscience and Religion. Plymouth, UK: Lexington Books, 2009.

Gazzaniga, M. S. (1985). The social brain. New York: Basic Books.

Gazzaniga, M.S. (1993), 'Brain mechanisms and conscious experience', Ciba Foundation Symposium, 174.

Geschwind N. "Behavioural changes in temporal lobe epilepsy". Psychol Med. 1979.

Gellhorn, E., Kiely, W.F. "Mystical states of consciousness: neurophysiological and clinical aspects." J Nerv Ment Dis. 1972;154:399-405.

Gilbert SL, Dobyns WB, Lahn BT (2005) Genetic links between brain development and brain evolution. Nat Rev Genet 6.

Gray JA. The Psychology of Fear and Stress. 2nd ed. New York, NY: Cambridge University Press; 1988.

Gloor, P. (1992), 'Amygdala and temporal lobe epilepsy', in The Amygdala: Neurobiological Aspects of Emotion, Memory and Mental

Dysfunction, ed J.P. Aggleton (New York: Wiley-Liss).

Gross CG, Rocha-Miranda CE, Bender DB (1972) Visual properties of neurons in the inferotemporal cortex of the macaque. J Neurophysiol 35: 96–111.

Guevara Che, The Motorcycle Diaries, 1992

Hardy, G. H. (1940). Ramanujan. Cambridge: Cambridge University Press.

Hall, Daniel, Keith Meador, and Harold Koenig. "Measuring Religiousness in Health Research: Review and Critique." Journal of Religion and Health 47, no. 2 (2008)

Harris, Sam, Jonas Kaplan, Ashley Curiel, Susan Bookheimer, Marco Iacoboni, and Mark Cohen. "The Neural Correlates of Religious and Nonreligious Belief." PLoS One 4, no. 10 (October 1, 2009)

Halgren, E. (1992), 'Emotional neurophysiology of the amygdala within the context of human cognition', in The Amygdala: Neurobiological Aspects of Emotion, Memory and Mental Dysfunction, ed J.P. Aggleton (New York: Wiley-Liss).

Halligan PW, Fink GR, Marshal JC, Vallar G. 2003. Spatial cognition: evidence from visual neglect. Trends Cogn Sci.

Handbook of Emotions, Edited by Michael Lewis, Jeannette M. Haviland-Jones, and Lisa Feldman Barrett, The Guilford Press; 3rd edition (2010).

Hameroff, S.R. and Penrose, R. (1996) Conscious events as orchestrated space-time selections. Journal of Consciousness Studies 3(1), 36-53; also reprinted in J. Shear (ed.) (1997) Explaining Consciousness-The Hard Problem. Cambridge, MA, MIT Press, 177-95.

Harding, D.E. (1961) On Having no Head: Zen and the Re-Discovery of the Obvious. London, Buddhist Society.

Hardy, A. (1979) The Spiritual Nature of Man: A Study of Contemporary Religious Experience. Oxford, Clarendon Press.

Harre, R. and Gillett, G. (1994) The Discursive Mind. Thousand Oaks, CA, Sage.

Haugeland, J. (ed.) (1997) Mind Design II: Philosophy, Psychology, Artificial Intelligence. Cambridge, MA, MIT Press.

Hauser, M.D. (2000) Wild Minds: What Animals Really Think. New York, Henry Holt and Co.; London, Penguin.

Hilgard, E.R. (1986) Divided Consciousness: Multiple Controls in Human Thought and Action. New York, Wiley.

Hilton, E.N., Lundberg, T.R. Transgender Women in the Female Category of Sport: Perspectives on Testosterone Suppression and Performance Advantage. Sports Med 51, 199–214 (2021).

Hitler, Adolf. Mein Kampf, 1925

Hodgson, R. (1891) A case of double consciousness. Proceedings of the Society for Psychical Research 7, 221-58.

Hofstadter, D.R. and Dennett, D.C. (eds) (1981) The Mind's I: Fantasies and Reflections on Self and Soul. London, Penguin.

Holland, J. (ed.) (2001) Ecstasy: The Complete Guide: A Comprehensive Look at the Risks and Benefits of MDMA. Rochester, VT, Park Street Press.

Holmes, D.S. (1987) The influence of meditation versus rest on physiological arousal. In M. West (ed.)

The Psychology of Meditation. Oxford, Clarendon Press, 81-103.

Holmstrom, David. 1992, Christian Science Monitor

Holloway RL (1996) Evolution of the human brain. In: Lock A, Peters CR (eds) Handbook of human symbolic evolution. Oxford University Press, Oxford

Jeannerod M (1988) The neural and behavioural organization of goal-directed movements. Clarendon Press, Oxford.

Johnson-Frey SH, Maloof FR, Newman-Norlund R, Farrer C, Inati S, Grafton ST (2003) Actions or hand-objects interactions? Human inferior frontal cortex and action observation. Neuron 39: 1053–1058.

Jackson, F. (1982) Epiphenomenal qualia. Philosophical Quarterly 32, 127-36.

James, W. (1890) The Principles of Psychology (2 volumes). London, Macmillan.

James, W. (1902) The Varieties of Religious Experience: A Study in Human Nature. New York and London, Longmans, Green and Co.

Jansen, K. (2001) Ketamine: Dreams and Realities. Sarasota, FL, Multidisciplinary Association for Psychedelic Studies.

Jay, M. (ed.) (1999) Artificial Paradises: A Drugs Reader. London, Penguin.

Jaynes, J. (1976) The Origin of Consciousness in the Breakdown of the Bicameral Mind. New York, Houghton Mifflin.

Kandel, E. R. In Search of Memory: The Emergence of a New Science of Mind, W. W. Norton & Company (2007).

Kandel E. R. Schwartz JH, Jessel TM. Principles of neural sciences. New York; McGraw Hill, 2000.

Kanwisher, N. (2001) Neural events and perceptual awareness. Cognition 79, 89-113; also reprinted inS. Dehaene (ed.) The Cognitive Neuroscience of Consciousness. Cambridge, MA, MIT Press, 89-113.

Kihlstrom, J.F. (1996) Perception without awareness of what is perceived, learning without awareness of what is learned. In M. Velmans (ed.) The Science of Consciousness. London, Routledge, 23-46.

Kosslyn, S.M. (1980) Image and Mind. Cambridge, MA, Harvard University Press.

Kosslyn, S.M. (1988) Aspects of a cognitive neuroscience of mental imagery. Science 240, 1621-6.

Kjaer, Troels, Camilla Bertelsen, Paola Piccini, David Brooks, Jorgen Alving, and Hans Lou. "Increased Dopamine Tone during Meditation- Induced Change of Consciousness." Cognitive Brain Research 13, no. 2 (April 2002)

Kölmel HW. 1985. Complex visual hallucinations in the hemianopic field. J Neurol Neurosurg Psychiatry.

Koenig, Harold. "Research on Religion, Spirituality, and Mental Health: A Review." Canadian Journal of Psychiatry 54, no. 5 (May 2009)

Koenig, Harold, ed. Handbook of Religion and Mental Health. San Diego, CA: Academic Press, 1998

Kraepelin E. Psychiatry: A Textbook for Students and Physicians. New York, NY: Science History Publications; 1990.

Lauglin, Charles, John McManus, and Eugene d'Aquili. Brain, Symbol, and Experience. 2nd ed. New York: Columbia University Press, 1992

Lakoff, G. and M. Johnson (1999). Philosophy in the flesh. Basic Books: New York.

LeDoux, J. E. (1996). The emotional brain. New York: Simon & Schuster.

LeDoux, J.E. (1992), 'Emotion and the amygdala', in The Amygdala: Neurobiological Aspects of Emo- tion, Memory and Mental Dysfunction, ed J.P. Aggleton (New York: Wiley-Liss).

Levin, D.T. and Simons, D.J. (1997) Failure to detect changes to attended objects in motion pictures. Psychonomic Bulletin and Review 4, 501-6.

Levine,J. (1983) Materialism and qualia: the explanatory gap. Pacific Philosophical Quarterly 64, 354-61.

Levine,J. (2001) Purple Haze: The Puzzle of Consciousness. New York, Oxford University Press. Levine, S. (1979) A Gradual Awakening. New York, Doubleday.

Levinson, B.W. (1965) States of awareness during general anaesthesia. British Journal of Anaesthesia 37, 544-6.

Lewicki, P., Czyzewska, M. and Hoffman, H. (1987) Unconscious acquisition of complex procedural knowledge. Journal of Experimental Psychology: Learning, Memory and Cognition 13, 523-30.

Naskar, Abhijit. "What is Mind?", 2016

Naskar, Abhijit. "Love, God & Neurons: Memoir of A Scientist who found himself by getting lost", 2016

Naskar, Abhijit. "Principia Humanitas", 2017

Naskar, Abhijit. "We Are All Black: A Treatise on Racism", 2017

Naskar, Abhijit. "Either Civilized or Phobic: A Treatise on Homosexuality", 2017

Naskar, Abhijit. "Build Bridges not Walls: In the name of Americana", 2018

Naskar, Abhijit. "Citizens of Peace: Beyond the Savagery of Sovereignty", 2019

Naskar, Abhijit. "The Constitution of The United Peoples of Earth", 2019

Naskar, Abhijit. "Mission Reality", 2019

Naskar, Abhijit. "Good Scientist: When Science and Service Combine", 2020

Newberg, Andrew, and Jeremy Iversen. "The Neural Basis of the Complex Mental Task of Meditation: Neurotransmitter and Neurochemical Considerations." Medical Hypotheses 61, no. 2 (2003).

Newberg, Andrew. "How God Changes Your Brain: An Introduction to Jewish Neurotheology", CCAR

Journal: The Reform Jewish Quarterly, Winter 2016.

Newberg, Andrew, and Stephanie Newberg. "A Neuropsychological Perspective on Spiritual Development." In Handbook of Spiritual Development in Childhood and Adolescence, edited by Eugene Roehlkepartain, Pamela King, Linda Wagener, and Peter Benson. London: Sage Publications, Inc., 2005

Newberg, Andrew. "The Neurotheology Link An Intersection Between Spirituality and Health", Alternative and Complimentary Therapies, Vol 21 No 1, February 2015.

Newberg, Andrew, Nancy Wintering, Dharma Khalsa, Hannah Roggenkamp, and Mark Waldman. "Meditation Effects on Cognitive Function and Cerebral Blood Flow in Subjects with Memory Loss: A Preliminary Study." Journal of Alzheimer's Disease 20, no. 2 (2010)

Nash, M. (1995), 'Glimpses of the mind', Time.

Nesse RM. Proximate and evolutionary studies of anxiety, stress and depression: synergy at the interface. Neurosci Biobehav Rev. 1999;23:895-903.

Nicolelis, Miguel. (2011) "Beyond Boundaries: The New Neuroscience of Connecting Brains with Machines---and How It Will Change Our Lives", Times Books

O'Hara, K. and Scutt, T. (1996) There is no hard problem of consciousness. Journal of Consciousness Studies 3(4), 290-302, reprinted in J. Shear (ed.) (1997) Explaining Consciousness. Cambridge, MA, MIT Press, 69-82.

O'Regan, J.K. and Noe, A. (2001) A sensorimotor account of vision and visual consciousness. Behavioral and Brain Sciences 24(5), 883-917.

Ornstein, R.E. (1977) The Psychology of Consciousness (2nd edn). New York, Harcourt.

Ornstein, R.E. (1986) The Psychology of Consciousness (3rd edn). New York, Pehguin.

Ornstein, R.E. (1992) The Evolution of Consciousness. New York, Touchstone.

Penfield W, Faulk ME (1955) The insula: further observations on its function. Brain 78: 445– 470.

Penrose, R. (1994), Shadows of the Mind (Oxford: Oxford University Press).

Penrose, R. (1989), The Emperor's New Mind: Concerning Computers, Minds and The Laws of Physics (Oxford: Oxford University Press).

Persinger, "'I would kill in God's name' role of sex, weekly church attendance, report of a religious experience and limbic lability" Perceptual and Motor Skills 1997.

Persinger "Experimental simulation of the God experience" Neurotheology 2003.

Persinger, Corradini, Clement, Keaney, et al "Neurotheology and its convergence with neuroquantology" NeuroQuantology 2010.

Persinger. "The neuropsychiatry of paranormal experiences". J Neuropsychiatry Clin Neurosci 2001.

Persinger. "Neuropsychological bases of god beliefs", New York: Praeger, 1987

Persinger. "Temporal lobe epileptic signs and correlative behaviors displayed by normal populations", Journal of General Psychology, 1986

Perry BD, Pollard R. Homeostasis, stress, trauma, and adaptation. A neurodevelopmental view of childhood trauma. Child Adolesc Psychiatr Clin N Am. 1998;7:33.

Ramachandran VS. Behavioral and magnetoencephalographic correlates of plasticity in the adult human brain. Proc Natl Acad Sci USA 1993; 90: 10413–20.

Ramachandran VS. Plasticity and functional recovery in neurology. Clin Med 2005; 5: 368–73.

Rock I, Victor J. Vision and touch: an experimentally created conflict between the two senses. Science 1964; 143: 594–6.

Roberts, TA; Smalley, J; Ahrendt, D (December 2020). "Effect of gender affirming hormones on athletic performance in transwomen and transmen: implications for sporting organisations and legislators". British Journal of Sports Medicine. 55 (11): 577–583

Royet JP, Plailly J, Delon-Martin C, Kareken DA, Segebarth C (2003) fMRI of emotional responses to odors: influence of hedonic valence and judgment, handedness, and gender. Neuroimage 20: 713–728.

Rozin R Haidt J and McCauley CR (2000) Disgust. In: Lewis M, Haviland-Jones JM (eds) Handbook of Emotion. 2nd Edition. Guilford Press, New York, pp 637–653.

Saxe R, Carey S, Kanwisher N (2004) Understanding other minds: linking developmental psychology and functional neuroimaging. Annu Rev Psychol 55: 87–124.

S. J. Russell and P. Norvig, Artificial intelligence: a modern approach (3rd edition): Prentice Hall, 2009.

Singer T, Seymour B, O'Doherty J, Kaube H, Dolan RJ, Frith CD (2004) Empathy for pain involves the affective but not the sensory components of pain. Science 303: 1157–1162.

Smith A (1759) The theory of moral sentiments (ed. 1976). Clarendon Press, Oxford.

Schilling, Vincent. 2017, indian country today

Stein, Stephen K. 2017, The Sea in World History: Exploration, Travel, and Trade

Tesla N. "My Inventions", 1919

T. R. Society, "Machine learning: the power and promise of computers that learn by example," ed. The Royal Society, 2017.

Tomasello M, Call J (1997) Primate cognition. Oxford University Press, Oxford

www.ingramcontent.com/pod-product-compliance
Lightning Source LLC
Chambersburg PA
CBHW051051250726
48656CB00001B/254